Toastmaster's Guide:

Crafting Unforgettable Wedding Toasts

By Greig Borthwick

DEDICATION

To all the people that have been tasked with
creating a memorable wedding moment.
Here's to not fucking it up!

CONTENTS

ACKNOWLEDGMENTS

I created this guide to hand out to all the people my fiancé has tasked to do speeches at our wedding. I wanted to make sure this day was memorable in every way. I figured it could be useful to so many others.

Chapter 1:
The Power of Wedding Toasts

Understanding the Significance of Wedding Toasts

A wedding is a milestone in the lives of two people who are committing to share their lives together. It represents the culmination of their love story and the beginning of a new chapter filled with shared dreams, challenges, and joys. Wedding toasts, often delivered during the reception, are an integral part of this celebration. In this chapter, we'll delve deeper into the importance and significance of wedding toasts in the context of this beautiful occasion.

A Symbol of Celebration

Toasting, in the context of a wedding, serves as a powerful symbol of celebration. When you raise your glass to honor the newlyweds, you're not just participating in a tradition; you're actively engaging in the joyful atmosphere of the event. This simple gesture signifies your recognition and appreciation of the love and commitment the couple has for each other.

A Moment of Connection

Weddings are gatherings of friends and family, often from diverse backgrounds and with varying degrees of familiarity with the couple. Wedding toasts create a unique opportunity for these individuals to connect with one another. As you stand up to deliver a toast, you're not only addressing the couple; you're reaching out to everyone present, inviting them to join in the celebration. Your words, filled with love and well-wishes, serve as a bridge that connects people, no matter how different their lives might be.

Emotional Significance

One of the most remarkable aspects of wedding toasts is the emotional depth they bring to the celebration. Your words have the power to evoke genuine emotions in both the couple and the guests. As you share your thoughts and blessings, you have the potential to bring tears of joy to the couple's eyes and create a warm, emotional atmosphere in the room. Your toast can be a heartwarming and memorable moment, leaving a lasting impression on everyone present.

History and Evolution

Toasts at weddings have a rich history, steeped in tradition. In the past, they served various practical purposes, such as ensuring the drinks were not poisoned. Over time, they evolved into an expression of goodwill and support. Today, they are a central part of wedding celebrations, representing the love and affection of those who raise their glasses. Understanding the history and evolution of wedding toasts provides a deeper appreciation for their significance in modern weddings.

Toast as a Symbol of Celebration

The act of toasting has a rich and diverse history, spanning various cultures and time periods. It has been a symbol of celebration and goodwill for centuries, and when incorporated into a wedding, it carries profound significance.

A Global Tradition

Toasting as a tradition is not confined to any one culture; it is a universal practice. Throughout history, people have raised their glasses to celebrate important moments, and weddings are among the most cherished of these occasions. While the specifics of toasting ceremonies may vary, the underlying sentiment remains the same: it's an expression of joy, goodwill, and hope.

Symbolizing Unity and Well-Wishes

When you raise your glass in a toast at a wedding, you're not only acknowledging the love and commitment of the couple, but you're also symbolically joining in their journey. The clinking of glasses, the uplifting of spirits, and the words spoken during a toast all come together to create a unique atmosphere of unity and celebration.

An Act of Respect and Honor

In many cultures, toasting is an act of respect and honor. It signifies that the couple's union is a momentous event deserving of recognition and celebration. Toasts demonstrate that the guests are not merely attendees but active participants in the couple's happiness.

A Time-Honored Tradition

The tradition of toasting at weddings dates back centuries. From medieval European banquets to ancient Chinese wedding feasts, the act of raising a glass to honor the newlyweds has endured the test of time. In each culture, it has been a way to convey well-wishes, offer blessings, and share in the joy of the couple.

A Joyful Rite of Passage

Weddings are rites of passage, marking the transition from one phase of life to another. The act of toasting symbolizes this transition and, in doing so, adds an extra layer of joy and festivity to the occasion. It represents the couple's journey into a shared life together, filled with hope and happiness.

Cultivating an Atmosphere of Celebration

Understanding the deep-rooted tradition of toasting is essential for anyone participating in a wedding toast. Whether you're the best man, maid of honor, a close friend, or a family member, your words and actions during the toast contribute to the atmosphere of celebration and unity that defines a wedding.

Incorporating this knowledge into your toast can help you appreciate the significance of the moment and convey your heartfelt well-wishes to the couple. It's not just a matter of following a tradition; it's about actively engaging in the celebration of love, unity, and commitment that a wedding represents.

A Moment of Connection

Wedding toasts, in addition to celebrating the love and commitment of the couple, offer a unique opportunity for guests to come together, share in the couple's happiness, and express their support and good wishes. This chapter explores the idea that toasting is not just a formality but a powerful vehicle for fostering connection and unity among those present at the wedding.

The Unity of the Gathering

A wedding is a gathering of people from various corners of the couple's lives, often spanning different social circles, generations, and backgrounds. It's a rare occasion where friends and family, some of whom may not have met before, come together to celebrate a shared love. Wedding toasts, delivered by select individuals, serve as a means to unite the diverse guest list.

Shared Emotions and Sentiments

As the toastmaster, you're not just addressing the couple; you're speaking on behalf of everyone in the room. Your words convey not only your feelings but the collective sentiments of the guests. It's a moment of collective joy, and the toast amplifies the emotional resonance in the room.

An Invitation to Connect

During a wedding toast, the focus is not solely on the toastmaster or the couple; it extends to every guest. When you raise your glass and look around, you're inviting others to join in the celebration. Your gesture encourages everyone to participate actively, regardless of their familiarity with the couple or the other guests.

The Role of Engagement

A wedding is not a passive event. It's an occasion that thrives on active engagement, whether it's through dancing, laughter, or heartfelt conversations. Wedding toasts are a key component of this engagement. They require attention, empathy, and a willingness to be part of the moment, and they contribute to the overall success of the celebration.

Creating Lasting Connections

Wedding toasts have the potential to forge connections that endure beyond the wedding day. People who might have been strangers find common ground and shared experiences. The toast becomes a conversation starter, allowing guests to reminisce about the sentiments expressed and the love felt in the room.

A Celebration of Life and Love

In the grand tapestry of life, wedding toasts are threads that weave together the stories of the couple and their guests. They celebrate not only the union of two individuals but the bonds that connect the couple to their friends and family. Each toast is a reminder of the shared moments, emotions, and love that make life rich and fulfilling.

Inclusivity and Unity

As you craft and deliver your wedding toast, remember that you have the opportunity to foster inclusivity and unity among the guests. You're not just raising your glass to the couple; you're extending an invitation for everyone to be part of the celebration. It's a powerful moment of connection that transcends words and extends into the shared experience of love, unity, and celebration.

Emotional Significance

Wedding toasts are not just words spoken into the air; they are profound expressions of love, support, and best wishes. In this chapter, we'll delve into the emotional significance of wedding toasts and how a well-crafted and heartfelt toast can evoke tears of joy and warmth in both the couple and the guests.

A Depth of Feeling

Weddings are inherently emotional events. They mark the culmination of a deep, loving relationship and the beginning of a shared life journey. A wedding toast allows you to tap into these emotions and share your feelings openly. The words you choose can convey the depth of your love, admiration, and support for the couple.

Tears of Joy

A well-delivered toast has the power to evoke tears of joy. When your words resonate with the couple and the guests, they become more than just a formality; they become a source of genuine happiness. The couple's love and commitment shine through, and the emotions that well up in response are often tears of pure, unadulterated joy.

Creating a Memorable Moment

A heartfelt toast has the potential to create a truly memorable moment. When you speak from the heart, your words become etched in the memories of the couple and the guests. These are the moments that people cherish long after the wedding day has passed, and they become a part of the couple's love story.

Warmth and Comfort

Warmth and comfort are often byproducts of a heartfelt toast. Your words can provide reassurance and comfort to the couple as they embark on this new chapter of their lives. The guests, too, feel the warmth of the occasion, knowing that their presence and support are valued.

The Power of Connection

An emotional toast can forge a strong connection between the couple and the guests. When your words resonate with the experiences and feelings of those in the room, it creates a sense of unity and shared emotions. It's not just about witnessing the couple's love; it's about actively participating in the celebration.

A Touching Tribute

A heartfelt toast is, in many ways, a tribute to the couple's love and the life they are building together. It's an acknowledgment of their journey, a celebration of their future, and a promise of continued support and love from their friends and family.

Your Role in Eliciting Emotion

As the person delivering the toast, you have a significant role in eliciting these emotions. Your words, tone, and sincerity can create an emotional atmosphere that envelops the room. It's not just about what you say; it's about how you say it. The way you deliver your toast, the genuine warmth in your voice, and the connection you establish with the couple and the guests all contribute to the emotional significance of the moment.

History and Evolution of Wedding Toasts

The tradition of wedding toasts has a fascinating history that has evolved over centuries. We will explore the origins of wedding toasts and their evolution into modern-day expressions of love and support.

Origins as a Gesture of Safety

The practice of toasting has its origins in ancient civilizations, dating back to the Greeks and Romans. It was customary to raise a glass and offer a toast to ensure the safety of the drinker. This tradition eventually found its way into wedding ceremonies as a symbolic act to ensure the well-being of the couple.

In medieval Europe, toasting had a practical purpose. It was believed that the clinking of glasses and the splashing of wine would drive away evil spirits that might pose a threat to the newlyweds. Thus, the first wedding toasts were more about protecting the couple from harm than expressing love and support.

The Rise of Symbolism and Good Luck

Over time, the act of toasting became more symbolic. People began to associate toasts with good luck and blessings for the future. It was no longer just a matter of ensuring the safety of the couple but also a way of invoking positive wishes for their life together.

Toasting vessels and special toasting goblets became popular, often adorned with intricate designs and inscriptions. These vessels were not only functional but also served as symbols of the couple's unity and the guests' well-wishing.

The Expression of Love and Support

As societies evolved and wedding traditions changed, the purpose of toasting shifted from a symbolic act of protection to an expression of love and support. Wedding toasts gradually became an opportunity for friends and family to convey their heartfelt blessings and congratulations to the newlyweds.

The content of the toasts evolved as well. Instead of focusing solely on well-being, toasts began to include expressions of love, hopes for a happy future, and anecdotes about the couple's journey together. These toasts became a way to celebrate the couple's love and commitment.

Modern-Day Wedding Toasts

Today, wedding toasts are a central part of wedding receptions. They have moved far beyond their origins as protective rituals and even beyond the simple expression of goodwill. Modern wedding toasts encompass a wide range of emotions and sentiments. They are a chance for friends and family to share personal stories, offer advice, and express their love and support for the couple.

Wedding toasts have also become more personalized, reflecting the unique qualities and experiences of the couple. They can be humorous, emotional, or a combination of both, depending on the personalities and preferences of the couple and the toastmaster.

Chapter 2:
Preparing for Your Toast

A well-prepared toast can make a significant difference in the overall experience of a wedding celebration. In this section, we'll explore the importance of planning your toast in advance and offer tips for crafting a meaningful and memorable speech.

Tips for Planning Your Toast in Advance

1. **Start Early:** Begin your preparations well in advance of the wedding day. This allows you ample time to brainstorm, write, edit, and rehearse your toast. Rushing at the last minute can lead to unnecessary stress.
2. **Understand Your Audience:** Consider the composition of the wedding guests. Think about their relationships with the couple, their

cultural backgrounds, and their preferences. Tailoring your toast to the audience ensures it will resonate with those present.

3. **Gather Stories and Anecdotes:** Collect stories, anecdotes, and memories related to the couple. Personal stories or experiences you've shared with them can add depth and authenticity to your toast.

4. **Structure Your Toast:** Create a clear structure for your toast. Typically, a good structure includes an introduction, body, and conclusion. Decide on the key points you want to cover, and organize your thoughts accordingly.

5. **Find a Theme or Message:** Identify a central theme or message for your toast. It could be about love, partnership, the couple's journey, or their qualities. Having a clear message will help guide your speech.

6. **Be Concise:** Keep your toast relatively short, typically lasting between two to five minutes. Guests may lose interest if the toast goes on for too long. Choose your words carefully to convey your message succinctly.

7. **Practice Out Loud:** Rehearse your toast multiple times. Speaking your

words aloud helps you refine your delivery, work out any stumbling points, and ensures that you're comfortable with the content.

8. **Seek Feedback:** Share your draft with a trusted friend or family member for feedback. They can offer suggestions for improvement and provide an outsider's perspective.

9. **Avoid Inside Jokes:** While personal anecdotes are great, avoid inside jokes that only a select few will understand. Your toast should be inclusive and relatable to all the guests.

10. **Edit and Refine:** After practicing and receiving feedback, edit your toast for clarity and brevity. Make sure your words are well-chosen, and your message is clearly conveyed.

The Role of the Toastmaster or Emcee

In many weddings, there's a designated toastmaster or emcee responsible for coordinating the order of toasts and introductions. If you're the designated toastmaster or emcee, here are some important considerations:

1. **Understand the Schedule:** Familiarize yourself with the wedding schedule, including when to introduce toasts, who will be giving them, and in what order.
2. **Communicate with Speakers:** Connect with the individuals giving toasts beforehand to confirm their readiness, the order of their speeches, and any specific details they'd like you to mention.
3. **Facilitate Transitions:** Smoothly transition between toasts and other parts of the reception. Maintain a sense of flow and keep guests informed about what's happening.
4. **Manage Timing:** Keep track of the time to ensure the event stays on schedule. If a toast is going on too long, gently signal to the speaker that it's time to wrap up.
5. **Offer Encouragement:** Provide words of encouragement to the speakers before they take the microphone. Reducing their nervousness can result in more confident and heartfelt toasts.

6. **Adapt to Changes:** Be prepared to handle unexpected changes or challenges during the toasting portion of the reception. Flexibility is key.

By planning your toast well in advance and understanding the role of the toastmaster or emcee, you can contribute to a seamless and memorable wedding celebration.

CHAPTER 3:
STRUCTURE AND CONTENT

The structure and content of your wedding toast are crucial to creating a memorable and meaningful speech. In this section, we'll explore the elements of a well-structured toast, including crafting the perfect opening and closing lines, incorporating personal stories and anecdotes, and achieving the right balance between humor and sentiment.

Opening Lines

The opening lines of your wedding toast are your chance to capture the attention of the audience and set the tone for your speech. They should be warm, inviting, and establish a connection with the guests. Here are three different approaches for opening lines:

1. **Express Gratitude:**
   - "Ladies and gentlemen, if I could ask you to raise your glasses, I'd like to start by expressing my heartfelt gratitude. Thank you to [Hosts' Names] for inviting me to speak today, and thank you to [Couple's Names] for allowing us all to share in this beautiful moment."

2. **Set the Tone:**
   - "Good evening, everyone! They say that love is the greatest adventure, and tonight, we're here to celebrate [Couple's Names] as they embark on the most epic journey of their lives."

3. **Introduce Yourself:**
   - "Hello, I'm [Your Name], and I have the pleasure of knowing [Bride's Name/Groom's Name/Couple's Names] [Specify your relationship]. Today, I'm honored to stand before you to toast this remarkable couple as they begin this new chapter in their lives."

These opening lines can serve as a strong foundation for your toast, and you can customize them to match your own style and the specific mood you want to create for the speech. Remember to speak from the heart and make a genuine connection with your audience from the very beginning.

Closing Lines

The closing lines of your wedding toast should leave a lasting and heartwarming impression. They are your opportunity to offer well-wishes, blessings, and a final toast to the couple. Here are three different approaches for closing lines:

1. **Raise a Toast:**
   - "So, if you'll all join me in raising your glasses, let's toast to [Couple's Names]. May their love shine brighter with each passing day, and may their journey together be filled with laughter, joy, and countless beautiful memories."
2. **Offer Blessings:**
   - "As we wrap up, I'd like to leave [Couple's Names] with a blessing.

May your love be as boundless as the oceans, as enduring as the mountains, and as beautiful as the stars in the sky. May your days be filled with happiness, and may your years be rich with love and laughter."

3. **End with Love:**
   - "In closing, let me simply say this: [Bride's Name and Groom's Name], your love has touched all of our hearts today. May it continue to grow, to inspire, and to be a beacon of light in your lives. We love you both, and we're so grateful to be a part of your beautiful journey."

These closing lines should reflect the essence of your toast and leave the couple and the guests with a sense of love, hope, and warmth. You can choose the approach that resonates most with your feelings and the tone of your speech. Remember, sincerity is key in delivering a heartfelt closing.

Including Personal Stories and Anecdotes

Incorporating personal stories and anecdotes into your wedding toast can add a heartfelt and authentic touch to your speech. Here are some tips to effectively include these anecdotes:

1. **Choose Relevant Stories:**
   - When selecting stories, focus on those that are meaningful and relevant to the couple's journey. Stories about how they met, memorable experiences they've shared, or moments that define their relationship are excellent choices.

2. **Keep It Concise:**
   - While personal stories are valuable, it's important to keep them concise. Avoid lengthy narratives that might lose the interest of the audience. Instead, focus on the essence of the story and the emotions it conveys.

3. **Highlight Key Moments:**
   - Use anecdotes to highlight key moments that capture the essence of the couple's relationship. Whether it's a humorous or heartwarming story, ensure it aligns with the overall message and

tone of your toast. These moments should provide insights into the couple's love, personalities, and the journey they've embarked on together.

4. **Engage the Audience:**
   - When sharing stories, aim to engage the audience. Use descriptive language, vivid details, and a conversational tone to draw in your listeners. By painting a picture with your words, you can help the guests connect with the couple's journey and the emotions you're trying to convey.

To illustrate these tips, let's consider an example of how to incorporate a personal story into a wedding toast:

Example: *"I vividly remember the day [Bride's Name] and [Groom's Name] first crossed paths. It was at [Describe the setting or event]. [Provide a concise description of the moment or interaction]. Little did we know that this chance encounter would set in motion a beautiful love story that continues to inspire us all. It's a testament to the power of fate and the enduring bond between these two incredible individuals."*

In this example, a relevant and concise story is shared, drawing the audience into the couple's journey and emphasizing the essence of their love. By doing so, you create a more personal and engaging toast that resonates with the couple and their guests.

Balancing Humor and Sentiment

Balancing humor and sentiment in your wedding toast is essential to create a well-rounded and memorable speech. Here are some tips to achieve this balance effectively:

1. **Know Your Audience:**
   - Consider the personalities of the couple and the preferences of the guests. Tailor your approach to suit the atmosphere and expectations of the event. For example, if the couple and guests have a playful sense of humor, you might incorporate more humor into your toast.
2. **Humor with Respect:**

- Inject humor but be respectful. Avoid jokes that could be offensive or embarrassing to the couple or any of the guests. Humor should bring smiles and laughter, not discomfort or offense. It's important to strike a balance where the humor is light-hearted and in good taste.

3. **Use Anecdotes:**
   - Personal anecdotes often carry both humor and sentiment simultaneously. Sharing a funny story from the couple's past can bring both laughter and emotional warmth to your toast. These anecdotes can be relatable and endearing to the audience.

4. **Balance Throughout:**
   - Strive for a balance between humor and sentiment throughout your toast. This might involve mixing humorous anecdotes with heartfelt blessings or reflections on the couple's love. You can start with a sentimental tone, introduce humor in the middle to lighten the mood, and then close on a heartfelt note.

5. **Timing is Key:**

- Consider the timing of your humorous elements, as it can affect the overall impact of your toast. For example, you might start with a sincere message to set the tone, insert humor to entertain and engage the audience, and conclude with heartfelt blessings and well-wishes.

To illustrate these tips, here's an example of how to balance humor and sentiment in a wedding toast:

"As I stand here today, I can't help but think of all the wonderful moments I've shared with [Bride's Name] and [Groom's Name]. [Share a humorous anecdote about the couple]. But beyond the laughter, I've witnessed the profound love and unwavering support that they provide to each other. It's a love that's as deep as it is beautiful, and I have no doubt that it will carry them through a lifetime of happiness and joy."

In this example, humor is introduced through an anecdote, and it is balanced with a heartfelt message that underscores the love and support between the couple. By finding the right balance between humor and sentiment, you can create a wedding toast that resonates with the couple and their guests and leaves a lasting impact.

Chapter 4:
Cultural Considerations

Wedding toasts are deeply influenced by cultural traditions and norms. Understanding and respecting these cultural considerations is essential when giving a wedding toast, especially in diverse settings. Here, we'll explore some toasting traditions from around the world and how to navigate diverse cultural backgrounds.

Toasting Traditions from Around the World

Toasting traditions vary widely across different cultures, and they add a unique and meaningful element to wedding celebrations. Here are some toasting traditions from around the world:

Chinese Wedding Toasts:

In Chinese weddings, toasts are a central part of the celebration. Guests offer toasts to the couple during the banquet, and the couple reciprocates. It's customary to say "Ganbei," which means "dry glass," encouraging the guest to finish their drink. This tradition reflects well-wishing and a joyful atmosphere.

French Wedding Toasts:

In France, toasting is accompanied by the clinking of glasses, a universal symbol of celebration. Guests often shout "Vive les mariés!" which means "Long live the newlyweds!" to express their happiness for the couple. It's also common for guests to shout "Bis" to request another kiss from the couple, adding a playful element to the toasting tradition.

Jewish Wedding Toasts:

Jewish weddings are rich in tradition, and the breaking of the glass during the ceremony is a well-known practice. Following this symbolic act, a toast with the words "Mazal Tov" is often raised. "Mazal Tov" means "Congratulations" and is a joyful declaration of best wishes for the newlyweds.

Indian Wedding Toasts:

Indian weddings feature a variety of customs and rituals. Toasting often involves the exchange of garlands or flower leis between the couple and guests as a sign of respect and well-wishing. Guests may offer blessings for the couple's happiness and prosperity, often accompanied by joyful exclamations and singing.

African Wedding Toasts:

African wedding toasts vary by region and culture. In some African weddings, a "Kola nut" ceremony is a significant part of the celebration. Elders bless the couple and offer their well-wishes, and the couple's families often exchange Kola nuts as a sign of unity and respect.

Irish Wedding Toasts:

Irish weddings have a rich tradition of toasts and blessings. The most famous Irish wedding toast is "May the road rise to meet you," which is a wish for a prosperous and happy journey in life. Irish toasts often carry deep sentiment and reflect the importance of love, friendship, and good fortune.

These toasting traditions not only celebrate the couple's love and commitment but also reflect the cultural values and customs of each region. When giving a wedding toast in a multicultural setting, acknowledging, and respecting these traditions can enhance the overall experience and make the celebration even more meaningful.

Navigating Diverse Cultural Backgrounds

When delivering a wedding toast in a diverse cultural setting, consider the following tips to navigate cultural backgrounds effectively:

Research the Traditions: Familiarize yourself with the cultural traditions and customs related to toasting in the specific culture or region. Understanding the significance of these traditions can help you navigate them respectfully.
Respect Differences: Be mindful of the cultural differences and sensitivities in your audience. Some cultures may have strict customs or taboos around toasting, so it's important to respect these.

Incorporate Respectful Language:
When giving a toast, use language that aligns with the cultural context. If you are aware of specific phrases or blessings that are customary, consider incorporating them into your speech.

Ask for Guidance: If you're unsure about the customs, don't hesitate to ask the couple or a knowledgeable guest for guidance. They can provide valuable insights and help you navigate the event respectfully.

Keep It Inclusive: In diverse settings, aim to keep your toast inclusive and respectful of all backgrounds. Avoid favoring one culture over another, and express your best wishes in a way that resonates with a broad audience.

Understanding and respecting cultural considerations in wedding toasts is not only a sign of courtesy but also a way to make the celebration more meaningful and inclusive. By acknowledging and embracing the diverse cultural backgrounds present, you can create a toast that truly honors the couple and their guests.

Chapter 5:
Toasting Etiquette

Toasting etiquette is an important aspect of giving a wedding toast. It involves considerations such as the timing and order of toasts, as well as the appropriate use of props and multimedia. Following these guidelines can help ensure a smooth and memorable toasting experience.

Timing and Order of Toasts

Toasting at a wedding follows a customary order and timing to ensure that the reception proceeds smoothly. Here are guidelines for the timing and order of toasts:

Timing:

Toasts are usually given during the wedding reception, typically after the meal. Coordinate with the couple or the toastmaster to determine the exact timing for your toast. This ensures that your speech fits seamlessly into the program.

Order of Toasts:

The order of toasts may vary depending on cultural traditions and the preferences of the couple. However, a common sequence often includes:

Welcome Toast:

The host or emcee offers a welcome toast at the beginning of the reception. This serves as a gracious start to the festivities and expresses gratitude to all the guests for being present.

Father of the Bride:

Traditionally, the father of the bride offers a toast welcoming the groom into the family. He may also share sentimental thoughts about his daughter and express his best wishes for the couple.

Best Man and Maid of Honor:

The best man and maid of honor often follow with their toasts. These toasts typically include anecdotes and well-wishes for the couple. They can offer a more personal perspective on the bride and groom's relationship.

Other Toasts:

Additional toasts may follow, such as those from the groom, the bride, parents of the groom, or other close family and friends. These toasts provide an opportunity to share personal stories, blessings, or expressions of love and support for the couple.

Response from the Couple:

The newlyweds may choose to respond with a brief thank-you speech. They can express their gratitude, love, and appreciation for their guests. This response is a heartwarming way to conclude the series of toasts.

Coordination:

To ensure the reception flows smoothly, coordinate with the toastmaster or emcee. Be aware of the schedule and the order in which toasts will be given. Knowing when it's your turn to speak helps maintain the event's organization and ensures that toasts are delivered in an orderly manner.

Duration:

Keep your toast relatively short, typically lasting between two to five minutes. This duration ensures that your speech remains engaging and holds the interest of the guests.

Respect Timing:

Be mindful of the schedule and the need to keep the event on track. It's important not to exceed your allotted time, as doing so can disrupt the flow of the reception. Respect the time limit to maintain a seamless and enjoyable celebration.

Following the established order and observing timing guidelines for toasts allows you to contribute to a well-organized and harmonious wedding reception. It ensures that each toast is given the attention it deserves while maintaining the overall flow of the event.

Appropriate Use of Props and Multimedia

Incorporating props and multimedia into your wedding toast can add a unique and engaging element to your speech. Here are guidelines for using props and multimedia effectively:

Props:

Using props can be a creative and fun way to engage the audience and enhance your toast. Common props include photographs, items related to the couple's interests or hobbies, or sentimental objects. When using props, remember to do so tastefully and in a way that complements your message rather than distracting from it.

Multimedia:

Multimedia elements such as slideshows or videos can be a powerful and touching way to share memories and stories about the couple. If you plan to incorporate multimedia, consider the following:

a. **Equipment and Technical Support:** Ensure that the necessary equipment (e.g., projector, screen, laptop) is available and functioning properly. Test your presentation in advance to identify and resolve any potential technical glitches.

b. **Relevance:** The multimedia elements you include should be directly relevant to the couple's story and the overall message of your toast. Use photos, videos, or slides that support the sentiments and emotions you want to convey.

c. **Timing:** Coordinate the timing of your multimedia presentation with the emcee or toastmaster to ensure it flows smoothly within the program. It's important that the timing aligns with the overall schedule.

d. **Clarity and Visibility:** Ensure that the visuals and audio are clear and easily visible and audible to all guests, regardless of their seating position. Adjust the lighting and sound as needed to enhance the audience's experience.

Relevance:

The use of props and multimedia should enhance the sentiment and entertainment value of your toast. All elements, whether props or multimedia, should directly support and amplify the message you're conveying about the couple's love, journey, and the significance of the occasion.

Practice:

Rehearse the use of props and multimedia to ensure a seamless and impactful presentation. Become familiar with how to operate any equipment and anticipate potential issues. Additionally, have a backup plan in case of technical difficulties.

By following these guidelines, you can use props and multimedia effectively in your wedding toast, creating a memorable and engaging experience for the couple and their guests while ensuring that your message remains at the forefront of the presentation.

Chapter 6:
The Art of Storytelling

Storytelling is a powerful and essential element of delivering a memorable wedding toast. It allows you to connect with the audience, create emotional resonance, and share the couple's journey in a compelling way. Here's why storytelling is important in toasts and some tips for engaging the audience through storytelling:

Emotional Connection:

Stories have a unique power to evoke emotions. When you share meaningful stories about the couple's relationship, their milestones, or significant experiences, it creates a profound emotional connection between the audience and the couple. These emotions can range from joy and laughter to sentiment and love, making the toast deeply moving and heartfelt.

Relatability:

Stories make your toast relatable to the audience. When you weave personal stories into your speech, the guests can see themselves in the shared experiences. This relatability enables them to engage with and appreciate the couple's journey and love story on a more personal level.

Memorability:

People remember stories more vividly than they do facts, statistics, or general statements. Incorporating storytelling into your toast ensures that your message is not only heard but also retained. It's more likely to leave a lasting impression on the couple and their guests, who will recall the meaningful stories long after the wedding.

Entertainment:

Engaging stories add an element of entertainment to your toast. They captivate the audience's attention and maintain their focus on your words. Stories have the ability to entertain and delight, making the toast an enjoyable and memorable part of the celebration.

Tips for Engaging the Audience Through Storytelling:

Crafting a compelling wedding toast through storytelling requires skill and finesse. Here are some tips to engage the audience effectively:

Choose Relevant Stories:

Select stories that are closely related to the couple's relationship, journey, or moments that reflect their personalities and love. Relevance is key to making the story resonate with the audience.

Structure Your Story:

Organize your story with a clear beginning, middle, and end. Start by introducing the situation or setting the scene. Build tension or anticipation as you move through the narrative, and conclude with a meaningful message or insight that ties the story together.

Use Descriptive Language:

Paint a vivid picture with your words. Use descriptive language to help the audience visualize the scenes and connect with the emotions in the story. Create a sensory experience through your storytelling.

Inject Emotion:

Emotion is the heart of a good story. Whether it's joy, laughter, sentiment, or love, make sure your story carries the right emotional tone for your toast. Allow your own emotions to shine through as you speak.

Timing and Delivery:

Pay attention to the timing and delivery of your story. Ensure it flows seamlessly within the context of your speech and aligns with the overall structure of the toast. Use a natural, conversational tone when sharing the story to connect with the audience.

Engage the Senses:

Appeal to the audience's senses by describing sights, sounds, smells, and feelings associated with the story. This sensory engagement helps transport the listeners into the narrative, making the story more immersive.

Build Suspense or Anticipation:

If the story allows, create suspense or anticipation by withholding certain details until the right moment. This keeps the audience engaged and eager to hear more, adding an element of surprise and excitement to your toast.

Relatable Messages:

Conclude your story with a message or insight that is relatable to the couple and meaningful to the audience. This adds depth and relevance to your toast, leaving the audience with a valuable takeaway.

By harnessing the power of storytelling in your wedding toast, you create a speech that forges a deep emotional connection, enhances relatability, ensures memorability, and entertains the audience. These elements combine to make your toast a touching and unforgettable part of the wedding celebration.

Chapter 7:
Injecting Humor into Your Toast

Appropriate and Tasteful Humor:

Injecting appropriate and tasteful humor into your wedding toast can enhance the celebration while respecting the occasion and the couple's preferences. Here are some effective approaches to humor:

Know Your Audience:

Consider the personalities of the couple and the preferences of the guests. Tailor your humor to suit the atmosphere and expectations of the event. What might be funny to one group may not be to another, so understanding your audience is crucial.

Self-Deprecating Humor:

Self-deprecating humor involves making light-hearted jokes about yourself. This form of humor is typically safe and endearing. It allows you to add a touch of comedy without risking offense.

Light-Hearted Anecdotes:

Share light-hearted anecdotes or stories from the couple's journey that have a funny twist. These stories should be amusing but not embarrassing. They should celebrate the couple's relationship in a humorous and positive manner.

Puns and Wordplay:

Puns, wordplay, and clever humor that relate to the couple or the occasion can bring smiles to the audience without crossing boundaries. They often add a touch of whimsy and creativity to your toast.

Observational Humor:

Observational humor involves making light and relatable jokes that relate to the wedding, marriage, or love in general. This form of humor tends to be relatable and entertaining, engaging the audience with shared experiences and emotions.

The Dos and Don'ts of Wedding Comedy:

When incorporating humor into your wedding toast, it's essential to strike a balance between entertainment and respect for the occasion. Here are some dos and don'ts to guide your approach to wedding comedy:

Dos:

1. Be Respectful:

Always be respectful of the couple and their families. Avoid humor that could be seen as offensive or hurtful to any member of the audience. Maintain a tone that honors the significance of the occasion.

2. Practice Timing:

Ensure that your humorous elements are well-timed. Consider placing humor in the middle of your toast to lift the mood after a sentimental start and then closing on a heartfelt note. Timing is crucial to maintaining the right atmosphere.

3. Keep It Light:

Keep the humor light and positive. Avoid delving into dark or heavy subjects, controversial topics, or sensitive personal matters. Humor should be a source of joy and amusement for all.

4. **Rehearse Your Jokes:**

Practice your humorous lines to gauge how they'll be received. Consider sharing them with a trusted friend or family member to get feedback on their appropriateness. This external perspective can help you fine-tune your humor.

5. **Balance with Sentiment:**

Balance humor with sentiment. A successful wedding toast often combines humor and emotion, creating a well-rounded speech that touches hearts and brings smiles. The interplay between these elements enhances the overall impact of your toast.

Don'ts:

1. **Avoid Offensive Jokes:**

Refrain from telling jokes that are offensive, inappropriate, or potentially embarrassing to the couple, their families, or the guests.

Offensive humor can detract from the celebration and cause discomfort.

2. **Steer Clear of Controversy:**

Avoid humor that delves into controversial topics, such as politics, religion, or sensitive personal matters. These subjects can divide the audience and overshadow the joy of the occasion.

3. **Don't Overdo It:**

Excessive humor can overshadow the sentimental and meaningful aspects of the toast. Strive for a balance between humor and sentiment to ensure that both elements receive their due attention.

4. **Refrain from Inside Jokes:**

Inside jokes can alienate guests who are not familiar with the context. It's best to use humor that everyone can appreciate and understand, making the toast inclusive for all.

5. **Respect Cultural Sensitivities:**

Be mindful of cultural sensitivities and customs when using humor. What might be funny in one culture could be inappropriate in another. Show sensitivity to diverse backgrounds and traditions.

By adhering to these dos and don'ts, you can create a wedding toast that entertains and uplifts while maintaining respect for the couple, their families, and the significance of the occasion. Your humor will contribute to a memorable and joyous celebration.

By applying these approaches to humor, you can add a light and entertaining dimension to your wedding toast while ensuring that the humor is well-received and appropriate for the occasion. Remember that the key is to make people smile and enjoy the moment without causing offense or discomfort.

Chapter 8:
Adding Emotional Depth

Connecting with the Emotions of the Couple and Guests:

When delivering a wedding toast, creating an emotional connection with the couple and the guests is key to making your words resonate deeply. Here are some strategies to connect on an emotional level:

Acknowledge the Journey:

Begin by acknowledging the journey the couple has taken to reach this moment. Highlight the significance of their love story and the challenges they've overcome. Recognizing the path that has led them to this day adds depth to your toast.

Use Personal Connections:

Share personal stories or moments you've shared with the couple that reflect the depth of your connection and your understanding of their love. Personal anecdotes bring a sense of intimacy and authenticity to your toast.

Empathy and Empowerment:

Express empathy for the couple's experiences, both the joys and the trials they've encountered. Offer words of encouragement and support. Let them know that you understand the significance of their love and are there to support them on this journey.

Engage with the Audience:

Encourage the guests to connect emotionally by sharing stories, anecdotes, or sentiments that are relatable and touch their hearts. Create a sense of unity among the guests by using language that draws people into the emotions of the moment. Engaging the audience ensures that your toast resonates with a wider group.

Authenticity:

Be authentic and sincere in your words. Authenticity is a powerful tool in connecting with both the couple and the guests. Share your genuine feelings and experiences, and your words will carry more weight and emotional impact.

Expressing Well-Wishes and Blessings in Your Wedding Toast:

Conveying well-wishes and blessings in your wedding toast is a heartwarming way to celebrate the couple and offer them your love and support. Here are some key elements to consider when expressing your well-wishes and blessings:

Heartfelt Blessings:

Convey your well-wishes with heartfelt words. Offer sincere blessings that express your desire for the couple's happiness, love, and success in their journey together. Share your genuine hope that their life will be filled with joy and love.

Timeless Quotes or Verses:

Consider incorporating timeless quotes, verses, or blessings that hold special meaning for the couple or are universally recognized for their positive sentiments. These can add depth and significance to your toast, and they resonate with a broader audience.

Personalized Messages:

Craft a personalized message of love and support that is specific to the couple. Reflect on their unique qualities, aspirations, and journey. Your personalized message will demonstrate your understanding of the couple's relationship and your genuine care for their future together.

Positive Affirmations:

Use positive affirmations and uplifting words to inspire the couple and fill the room with hope and joy. Encourage them to embark on their new life together with confidence, love, and a sense of purpose. Positive affirmations can set a beautiful tone for their future.

Raise a Toast:

Conclude your toast by inviting all the guests to raise their glasses in a toast to the newlyweds. This traditional gesture signifies a collective expression of well-wishes and blessings. The act of raising a toast unites everyone in celebrating the couple's love and commitment.

By incorporating these elements into your wedding toast, you will create a memorable and touching moment that not only celebrates the couple but also leaves a lasting impression on the entire audience. Your words of well-wishes and blessings will add a meaningful and beautiful dimension to the celebration.

Chapter 9:
Delivering Your Toast with Confidence

Tips for Overcoming Public Speaking Anxiety:

Public speaking anxiety is common, but with the right strategies, you can manage it and deliver your wedding toast with confidence. Here are some tips to help you overcome anxiety:

Prepare Thoroughly:

The more you prepare and practice your toast, the more confident you will feel. Familiarize yourself with your speech, know your key points, and rehearse multiple times. Practice makes perfect, and confidence comes with competence.

Start with a Strong Opening:

Begin your toast with a strong and confident opening. A well-rehearsed opening can help set the tone for the entire speech and boost your confidence. An impactful start will capture the audience's attention and set a positive tone for the rest of your toast.

Breathe Deeply:

Deep breathing exercises can help calm your nerves. Before you start your toast, take a few deep breaths to center yourself and reduce anxiety. Deep breathing helps relax your body and mind, allowing you to speak more confidently.

Visualize Success:

Spend some time visualizing yourself delivering a successful toast. Positive visualization can help boost your confidence and reduce anxiety. Picture yourself speaking with poise and grace, and imagine the audience reacting positively to your words.

Use Notes Sparingly:

While it's helpful to have notes as a reference, try not to rely too heavily on them. Overreliance on notes can make you appear less confident. Instead, use bullet points or key phrases to jog your memory. This approach allows you to maintain better eye contact and engage with the audience.

Practice in Front of a Friend:

Rehearse your toast in front of a friend or family member who can provide feedback. This practice audience can help you get used to speaking in front of others and receive constructive input to improve your delivery.

By following these tips, you can build your confidence and effectively manage public speaking anxiety, ensuring that you deliver a heartfelt and memorable wedding toast.

Making Eye Contact and Projecting Your Voice:

When delivering a wedding toast, effective communication is crucial to ensure that your words are heard, understood, and felt by the audience. Here are some tips for making eye contact and projecting your voice with confidence:

Eye Contact:

Making eye contact with the audience and the couple is essential to convey sincerity and confidence. Connect with various guests by looking at different sections of the room. Avoid focusing solely on your notes or a single spot. Making eye contact creates a sense of engagement and connection.

Practice Eye Contact:

During your practice sessions, make a conscious effort to maintain eye contact with your practice audience. This will help you develop the habit of looking at your listeners, making it feel more natural when you deliver your toast. Practicing eye contact ensures that you come across as engaged and confident.

Voice Projection:

Speak clearly and project your voice so that everyone in the room can hear you. Practice your speech out loud to gauge your volume and clarity. Enunciate your words, and don't rush through your speech. Projecting your voice allows your words to reach every corner of the room, ensuring that your message is well-received.

Use Body Language:

Your body language can convey confidence and enthusiasm. Stand up straight, maintain good posture, and use hand gestures naturally to emphasize key points in your speech. Appropriate body language reinforces the message you're conveying and helps you appear more confident.

Control Nervous Habits:

Be aware of any nervous habits, such as fidgeting, pacing, or excessive hand movements. Try to control these habits during your toast to appear more composed and confident. Self-awareness and practice can help you minimize nervous gestures.

Pause and Breathe:

If you feel nervous or need a moment to collect your thoughts, it's perfectly acceptable to pause and take a breath. Pausing allows you to regain composure and speak with confidence. Deep breaths can also help calm your nerves and ensure a steady delivery.

Remember that some level of nervousness is normal, even for experienced speakers. The key is to manage your anxiety and build your confidence through thorough preparation and practice. By following these tips, you can deliver your wedding toast with confidence and make it a memorable and touching moment for the couple and the guests.

Chapter 10:
Examples and Samples

Sample Wedding Toast for Best Man:

Ladies and gentlemen, if I could have your attention, please.

I stand before you today not just as the best man but as someone who has had the immense privilege of witnessing the beautiful journey of [Bride's Name] and [Groom's Name] from the very beginning. And let me tell you, it's been nothing short of extraordinary.

From the moment they met, it was like the stars aligned and the universe conspired to bring these two incredible people together. Their love story is like a fairytale, and today, we celebrate the chapter where they say, "I do."

I've had the honor of being [Groom's Name]'s confidant, partner-in-crime, and, at times, his voice of reason. We've shared countless laughs, adventures, and memories. And throughout it all, I've seen him transform into the person he is today - a man who is unwaveringly dedicated to [Bride's Name] and the love they share.

[Bride's Name], you are not only radiant today but you've been a beacon of light in [Groom's Name]'s life. Your warmth, your kindness, and your unwavering support have touched us all. I've seen how you make each other better, and I couldn't be happier that my best friend has found the love of his life in you.

To the newlyweds, may your journey be filled with as much laughter, joy, and adventure as we've seen in your eyes today. May the love you have for each other continue to grow, and may every day of your life together be a testament to the strength of your love.

May you always remember that in each other's arms, you've found your home. And may the love that you share today and every day from this moment forward be as enduring as time itself.

So, ladies and gentlemen, please join me in raising your glasses to [Bride's Name] and [Groom's Name]. May their love be as infinite as the stars, and may their journey be filled with nothing but joy and love. Cheers to the newlyweds!

Sample Wedding Toast for Maid of Honor:

Ladies and gentlemen, family and friends,

Today, I have the honor of standing here as the Maid of Honor, and I am filled with joy as I raise my glass to celebrate the love between [Bride's Name] and [Groom's Name].

I have known [Bride's Name] for many years, and I can honestly say that she deserves all the happiness in the world. She's a person of incredible warmth, compassion, and grace. She's the kind of friend who will stand by you through thick and thin, and I have witnessed the depth of her love and devotion to [Groom's Name] from the very beginning.

[Groom's Name], you are a lucky man to have won [Bride's Name]'s heart. From the moment she met you, her eyes would light up with a special twinkle, and her smile would widen in a way I had never seen before. It was evident that you were the missing piece to her puzzle, the one who made her heart whole.

As I've watched your love story unfold, I've seen the countless ways you two complement each other. You balance each other in the most beautiful way, and your love has grown stronger with each passing day. Your journey together has been one of laughter, shared dreams, and unwavering support.

Today, we not only celebrate your love but also the promise of a beautiful future together. I have no doubt that your marriage will be filled with endless adventures, the warmth of shared laughter, and the strength that comes from supporting one another in all you do.

So, let us raise our glasses to [Bride's Name] and [Groom's Name], to the love they share, and to the beautiful journey that lies ahead. May your days be filled with love, your nights with joy, and your lives with countless memories that remind you of the remarkable love story you've created.

To [Bride's Name] and [Groom's Name], may your love be as endless as the stars in the sky and as enduring as the bond you share. Cheers!

Sample Wedding Toast for a Parent:

Ladies and gentlemen, family and friends,

As the proud parents of [Bride/Groom's Name], we stand before you today with hearts brimming with love and joy. We can't express how grateful we are to share this moment with all of you and to welcome [Spouse's Name] into our family.

From the very beginning, we've watched [Bride/Groom's Name] grow into the remarkable person they are today. We've seen them laugh, learn, and find their way in the world. But it's when they found [Spouse's Name] that their life took on a new and brighter dimension.

[Spouse's Name], from the moment you entered our lives, it was as if a missing piece of the puzzle had been found. You've brought boundless happiness to our child and to us as well. Your kindness, your love, and the way you make [Bride/Groom's Name] light up with joy have touched our hearts deeply.

Today, we're not losing a son or a daughter; instead, we're gaining another son/daughter. The bond of family grows, and our hearts are filled with gratitude for the love and joy that [Spouse's Name] brings into our lives.

As [Bride/Groom's Name]'s parents, our biggest wish has always been for their happiness, and seeing them with you, [Spouse's Name], makes our hearts sing. We know that the love you two share is special, enduring, and profound.

May your journey together be a tapestry of shared dreams, beautiful moments, and boundless love. May you always cherish and nurture the incredible connection you've built. May the laughter never fade, and may you find strength in each other during the challenges life may bring.

To [Bride/Groom's Name] and [Spouse's Name], may your love story continue to be a source of inspiration and joy. May the love you share today and every day be as enduring as the love we have for you.

Ladies and gentlemen, please join us in raising your glasses to [Bride/Groom's Name] and [Spouse's Name]. May your journey together be blessed with love, happiness, and a lifetime of cherished memories. Cheers to the newlyweds!

Sample Wedding Toast for a Close Friend:

Ladies and gentlemen, family, and friends,

Today, I have the extraordinary privilege of toasting two of the most extraordinary people I know - [Bride's Name] and [Groom's Name]. I've had the honor of being part of their journey from the moment they met, and I can say with absolute certainty that their love story is one for the books.

From the very beginning, it was clear that [Bride's Name] and [Groom's Name] were meant to be together. They share a connection that's not just built on love but on a deep understanding of one another. They're the kind of couple who brings out the best in each other, who make each other laugh until their sides hurt, and who are there for each other in both the brightest and darkest moments.

[Spouse's Name], you've managed to win not just the heart of [Bride's Name] but the hearts of all of us who have had the privilege of knowing you. Your kindness, your infectious spirit, and the love you've brought into [Bride's Name]'s life are truly special.

To the newlyweds, as you stand here today, you're not just making a commitment to one another, you're embarking on an incredible adventure together. And as your close friend, I couldn't be happier for the joy and love you've found in each other.

May your journey be filled with laughter, shared dreams, and a lifetime of memories. May the love you share continue to grow stronger with each passing day, and may your days be illuminated by the light of your love.

Ladies and gentlemen, please join me in raising your glasses to [Bride's Name] and [Groom's Name]. May your love story continue to be filled with happiness, laughter, and a love that knows no bounds. Cheers to the newlyweds!

Sample Wedding Toast for a Sibling:

Ladies and gentlemen, family and friends,

I stand before you today not just as [Bride's/Groom's Name]'s sibling but as someone who has had the incredible privilege of watching them grow and evolve. Today, I have the honor of toasting my sister/brother and the wonderful person they have chosen to share their life with.

From the day they met [Spouse's Name], I could see that something extraordinary was happening. Their connection, their laughter, and the way they've brought out the best in each other have been nothing short of magical. And it's this magic that brings us here today.

[Spouse's Name], from the moment you entered our lives, you became an integral part of our family. Your kindness, your warmth, and your boundless love for my sister/brother have touched our hearts deeply. We couldn't be happier that you've chosen to embark on this incredible journey together.

Today, we're not just gaining a new family member; we're gaining a dear friend and a partner in happiness. Your love has enriched our lives, and we can't thank you enough for that.

To [Bride's/Groom's Name] and [Spouse's Name], may your journey be filled with as much laughter, joy, and adventure as we've seen in your eyes today. May your love story continue to be as enchanting as it is today, and may you cherish every moment together.

May the love you share continue to grow, and may your days be filled with the kind of love that touches not only your hearts but the hearts of everyone around you.

Ladies and gentlemen, please join me in raising your glasses to [Bride's/Groom's Name] and [Spouse's Name]. May your love story continue to be an inspiration, and may your journey together be nothing short of extraordinary. Cheers to the newlyweds!

Sample Wedding Toast for a Colleague:

Ladies and gentlemen,

Today, I have the distinct honor of toasting not just a colleague but someone who has become a dear friend. I've had the privilege of working alongside [Bride's/Groom's Name] for some time, and today, I'm here to celebrate this incredible milestone in their life.

Working with [Bride's/Groom's Name] has been an enlightening experience. They're not just a dedicated and hardworking colleague, but they're also someone who knows how to bring positivity into any room. They have an extraordinary ability to inspire and uplift everyone around them.

And when [Bride's/Groom's Name] introduced me to [Spouse's Name], it was evident that something extraordinary was happening. [Spouse's Name], you've not only won [Bride's/Groom's Name]'s heart but the hearts of all of us who have had the pleasure of getting to know you.

Today, we're not just celebrating their love; we're celebrating the partnership, friendship, and shared dreams that [Bride's/Groom's Name] and [Spouse's Name] have built together.

May your journey be filled with as much enthusiasm, dedication, and love as you've put into your work and your lives. May your days be enriched with laughter, support, and shared achievements.

May the love you share be a source of inspiration not just for those present here but for all who know you. To [Bride's/Groom's Name] and [Spouse's Name], here's to a future filled with continued success, joy, and, most importantly, love.

Ladies and gentlemen, please join me in raising your glasses to [Bride's/Groom's Name] and [Spouse's Name]. May your love continue to inspire and shine as brightly as your careers. Cheers to the newlyweds!

Sample Wedding Toast for a Grandparent:

Ladies and gentlemen, family and friends,

Today, my heart is filled with immense joy as I stand before you to toast two remarkable young people, [Bride's Name] and [Groom's Name], and to celebrate their love and commitment. I am not just a grandparent but a witness to the beautiful journey of [Bride's Name]'s and [Groom's Name]'s lives.

To see the love that has blossomed between them warms my heart. It's a testament to the values we hold dear in our family - love, respect, and the unwavering support we offer one another. And as a grandparent, it brings me great happiness to see this love story unfold.

[Spouse's Name], you have not just won the heart of my grandchild but my heart as well. Your kindness, your warmth, and the love you bring into their life are truly special, and I feel blessed to have you as part of our family.

Today, as I stand here, I can't help but reflect on the beautiful journey of life, love, and family. [Bride's Name] and [Groom's Name], may your journey be as fulfilling and as beautiful as the love that you share today.

May your love be like a warm and constant flame, offering light and guidance as you traverse the path of life together. May you treasure each moment, lean on each other in times of need, and laugh together as you build your future.

Ladies and gentlemen, please join me in raising your glasses to [Bride's Name] and [Groom's Name]. May your love continue to grow stronger and may your days be filled with happiness, laughter, and the warmth of family. Cheers to the newlyweds!

Feel free to customize these sample toasts to fit your specific relationship and circumstances. Additionally, you can analyze these toasts for their elements, such as expressing well-wishes, personal anecdotes, and emotional connections, to understand what makes them successful.

Chapter 11:
Post-Toasting Etiquette

Mingling with guests is an essential part of post-toasting etiquette. Here are some additional tips to make the most of this time:

Share Your Warm Wishes:

Approach the couple and their families to offer your heartfelt congratulations. Sharing your warm wishes in person is a meaningful way to express your happiness for them.

Engage in Conversations:

Strike up conversations with other guests, whether you know them well or are meeting them for the first time. Celebrate the occasion, share stories, and get to know new people. Engaging with a diverse group of guests can enhance the overall experience.

Compliment the Hosts:

Don't forget to express your appreciation to the hosts of the wedding, who likely put in significant effort to make the day special. Thank them for including you in this joyous celebration.

Dance and Enjoy:

If there's dancing or other forms of entertainment, don't hesitate to join in. Show your enthusiasm and be part of the festivities. Celebrate, laugh, and make the event memorable for everyone.

Respect Cultural Norms:

Be aware of any cultural or religious customs that might influence interactions at the event. Demonstrating respect for these traditions can make a significant impression.

Remember, mingling with guests is not only an opportunity to celebrate but also a way to strengthen your connections and share in the joy of the newlyweds. Your presence and engagement can contribute to the overall success of the wedding celebration.

Following up with the newlyweds is a considerate way to continue your support and friendship. Here are some tips on how to do it effectively:

Send a Personal Message:

Reach out to the newlyweds with a personal message, whether it's in the form of a handwritten card or a heartfelt email. Express your happiness for them and let them know how much you enjoyed being part of their special day.

Reiterate Your Well-Wishes:

In your message, reiterate your well-wishes for their future together. You can mention the sentiments you shared during your toast and express your continued support and love.

Offer Assistance:

Let the newlyweds know that you're available to assist in any way they may need as they begin their journey as a married couple. Whether it's offering advice, helping with post-wedding tasks, or simply being there to listen, your support can be a source of comfort and joy for them.

Maintain Communication:

Keep the lines of communication open and check in with the couple periodically. Inquire about how they're adjusting to married life, ask about their plans, and show genuine interest in their happiness.

Respect Their Space:

While it's essential to be supportive, also respect the newlyweds' need for privacy and space as they navigate their post-wedding journey. Let them lead the way in how much they want to share and involve others.

By following up with the newlyweds, you not only extend your well-wishes but also reinforce the meaningful connection you share. Your continued friendship and presence can be a source of comfort, guidance, and joy for the newlyweds as they embark on this new chapter of their lives.

Chapter 12:
Additional Resources

Here are some additional resources and a list of popular toasting quotes and anecdotes to help you further improve your toasting skills and add depth to your wedding toasts:

Recommended Books:

1. "The Complete Book of Wedding Toasts" by Diane Warner
2. "Wedding Toasts I'll Never Give" by Ada Calhoun
3. "Wedding Toasts 101: The Guide to the Perfect Wedding Speech" by Peter Oxley

Websites:

1. **The Knot (theknot.com):** The Knot offers a variety of wedding-related tips, including guidance on writing and delivering toasts.
2. **WeddingWire (weddingwire.com):** WeddingWire provides resources on wedding speeches and toasts, including speech examples and tips.

Popular Toasting Quotes and Anecdotes:

1. "Love is not about how many days, months, or years you have been together. Love is about how much you love each other every single day." - Unknown
2. "True love stories never have endings." - Richard Bach
3. "Love is composed of a single soul inhabiting two bodies." - Aristotle
4. "The best thing to hold onto in life is each other." - Audrey Hepburn
5. "Love is not finding someone to live with; it's finding someone you can't imagine living without." - Rafael Ortiz
6. "Marriage is like a fine wine; it gets better with age." - Unknown
7. "The greatest happiness you can have is knowing that you are loved without conditions." - Jonathan Safran Foer
8. "A happy marriage is a long conversation which always seems too short." - Andre Maurois
9. "A good speech should be like a woman's skirt; long enough to cover the subject and short enough to create interest." - Winston S. Churchill

10.   "The best love is the kind that awakens the soul; that makes us reach for more, that plants the fire in our hearts and brings peace to our minds." - Nicholas Sparks

These resources and quotes can help you craft memorable wedding toasts that capture the essence of love and commitment. Remember to personalize your toasts and infuse them with your unique voice and heartfelt sentiments.

Chapter 13:
Final Thoughts

In closing, I encourage you to embrace the role of a toastmaster with enthusiasm and joy. Delivering a heartfelt wedding toast is not just an honor; it's an opportunity to make a lasting impact on a couple's most special day. Your words have the power to evoke emotions, create connections, and contribute to the beautiful memories that will be cherished for a lifetime.

Weddings are a celebration of love, unity, and commitment, and your toast plays a significant role in this celebration. It's a moment of connection, a display of affection, and a testament to the enduring power of love. When you raise your glass and offer your words of love, support, and blessings, you become a part of a beautiful love story that will continue to unfold.

The impact of a heartfelt wedding toast lingers long after the cheers have faded. It brings smiles, laughter, and sometimes tears of joy, creating a treasure trove of memories for the couple and their guests. Your words become woven into the fabric of their love story, a chapter that they will revisit again and again, finding comfort, inspiration, and joy in the sentiments you shared.

So, whether you're a best man, a parent, a close friend, a sibling, a colleague, or even a grandparent, embrace your role as a toastmaster with love and authenticity. Craft a toast that resonates with the couple and their guests, share stories that touch hearts, and raise your glass to celebrate the enduring power of love. Your heartfelt wedding toast is a gift that keeps on giving, leaving an indelible mark on the hearts of those you honor. Cheers to the beautiful journey of love and to the unforgettable moments that your toasts will create.

Appendix:
Toasting Quotes and Inspirational Stories

Quotes:

1. "Love isn't something you find. Love is something that finds you." - Loretta Young
2. "In all the world, there is no heart for me like yours. In all the world, there is no love for you like mine." - Maya Angelou
3. "Love is the flower you've got to let grow." - John Lennon
4. "Love is an endless act of forgiveness. Forgiveness is the key to action and freedom." - Maya Angelou
5. "To love and be loved is to feel the sun from both sides." - David Viscott

6. "A successful marriage requires falling in love many times, always with the same person." - Mignon McLaughlin
7. "Here's to love, laughter, and happily ever after." - Unknown
8. "May your love be modern enough to survive the times and old-fashioned enough to last forever." - Unknown
9. "A successful marriage is an edifice that must be rebuilt every day." - André Maurois
10. "To the bride and groom, may your love be as endless as your joy." - Unknown

Inspirational Stories:

1. The Tale of the Old Oak Tree: Share a story about an old oak tree that has stood the test of time, symbolizing the strength and endurance of love. Just as the tree weathers storms and seasons, love can grow stronger and more beautiful with each passing year.
2. The Grandparents' Love Story: Narrate a heartwarming story about the enduring love between the grandparents of the couple. This story can serve as an example of love's resilience and the

inspiration that lasting love can bring to the newlyweds.

3. The Journey of Two Souls: Tell a story about the couple's journey together, highlighting the moments that brought them closer and the challenges they've overcome. Emphasize the power of their love to conquer all obstacles.

4. The Wedding Day Rescue: Share a humorous anecdote about a wedding day mishap that was hilariously saved by quick thinking and teamwork. Use this story to illustrate how love and partnership can conquer any unexpected challenges.

These quotes and stories can add depth and emotion to your wedding toasts, helping you craft memorable speeches that touch the hearts of the couple and their guests. Remember to choose the ones that resonate most with the couple's journey and the sentiments you wish to convey.

www.ingramcontent.com/pod-product-compliance
Lightning Source LLC
Chambersburg PA
CBHW070814280726
48660CB00015B/503